Fantastic Cats

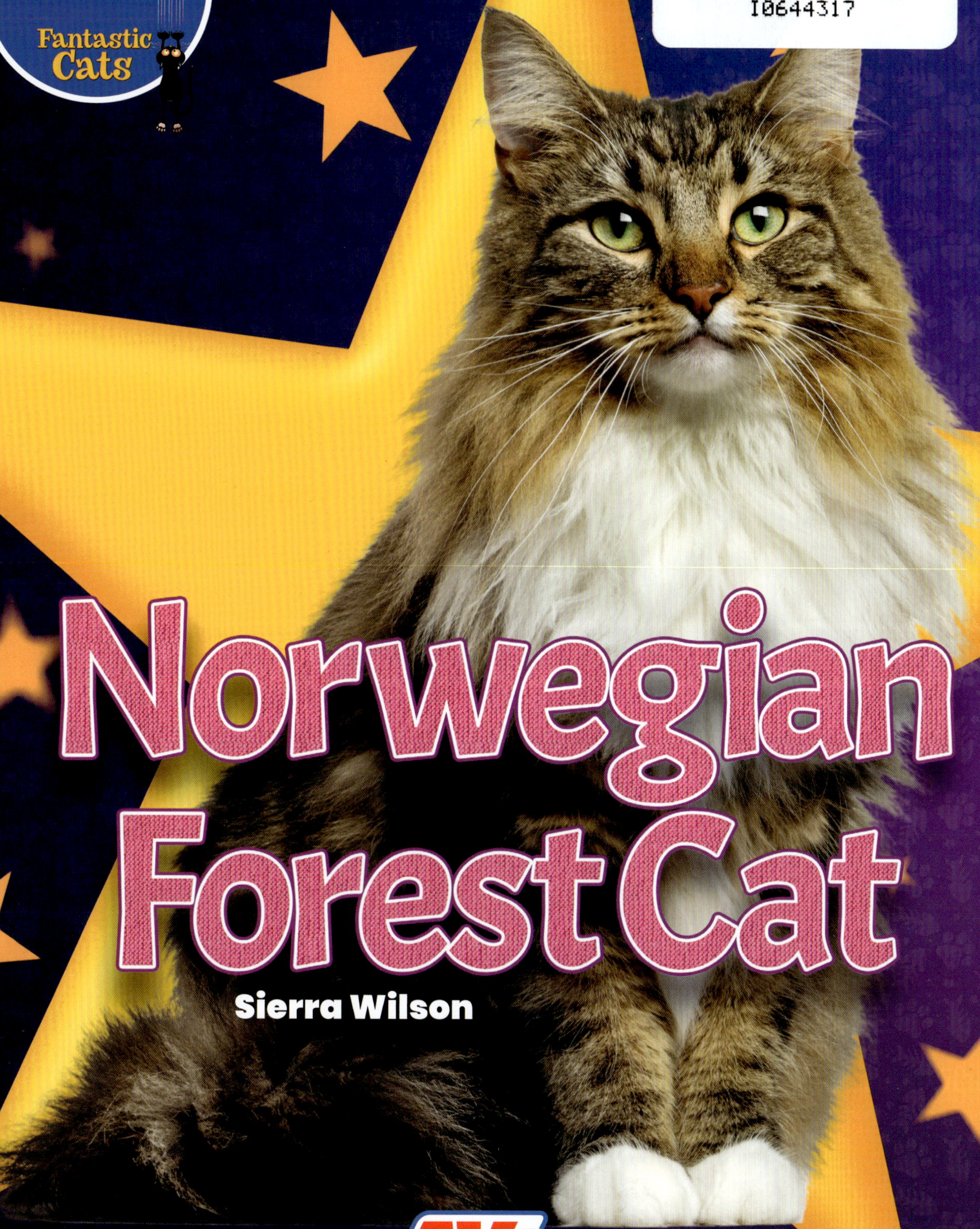

Norwegian Forest Cat

Sierra Wilson

AV2
www.openlightbox.com

Step 1
Go to www.openlightbox.com

Step 2
Enter this unique code
DNYLMNJQW

Step 3
Explore your interactive eBook!

AV2 is optimized for use on any device

Your interactive eBook comes with...

Contents
Browse a live contents page to easily navigate through resources

Audio
Listen to sections of the book read aloud

Videos
Watch informative video clips

Weblinks
Gain additional information for research

Slideshows
View images and captions

Try This!
Complete activities and hands-on experiments

Key Words
Study vocabulary, and complete a matching word activity

Quizzes
Test your knowledge

Share
Share titles within your Learning Management System (LMS) or Library Circulation System

Citation
Create bibliographical references following APA, CMOS, and MLA styles

This title is part of our AV2 digital subscription

1-Year K–5 Subscription
ISBN 978-1-7911-3320-7

Access hundreds of AV2 titles with our digital subscription.
Sign up for a FREE trial at www.openlightbox.com/trial

The digital components of this book are guaranteed to stay active for at least five years from the date of publication.

Fantastic Cats

Norwegian Forest Cat

Contents

Name the Cat

Which big, fluffy cat looks like it comes from the wild?

Which cat is the national cat of Norway?

Which cat is fully grown by 5 years of age?

The Norwegian Forest Cat!

Meet the Norwegian Forest Cat

Norwegian forest cats, or "Wegies," are large, friendly cats that love to be around people. They are popular cats around the world, but especially in their **native** Norway and throughout Northern Europe. Norwegian forest cats are built for the cold. They have fluffy fur with a **ruff** around their necks.

Norwegian forest cats enjoy a mixture of activity and relaxation. They like to climb, play, and explore. They also like to cuddle and simply spend time with their owners. Anyone looking for an easygoing family cat should take a look at this **breed**.

The Norwegian Forest Cat Breed

Norwegian forest cats are **fully grown** by **5 years** of age.

The Norwegian forest cat became **Norway's official cat breed** in the **1950s**.

Norwergian forest cats can live for up to **16 years**.

Norwegian Forest Cat History

The Norwegian forest cat breed developed naturally over hundreds of years in the cold forests of Norway. Over time, these cats became smart, tough animals that could handle freezing weather and other challenges. They were likely used by the **Vikings** to hunt **vermin** in their ships and homes.

By the 1900s, the breed had become rare and was almost lost. In the 1930s, cat lovers in Norway started to work together to save these cats. Their work paid off, and the Norwegian forest cat breed soon began to be known outside of Norway as well. An official breeding pair of Norwegian forest cats first came to the United States in 1979. The International Cat Association (TICA), an important **pedigree registry**, officially recognized the breed in 1984.

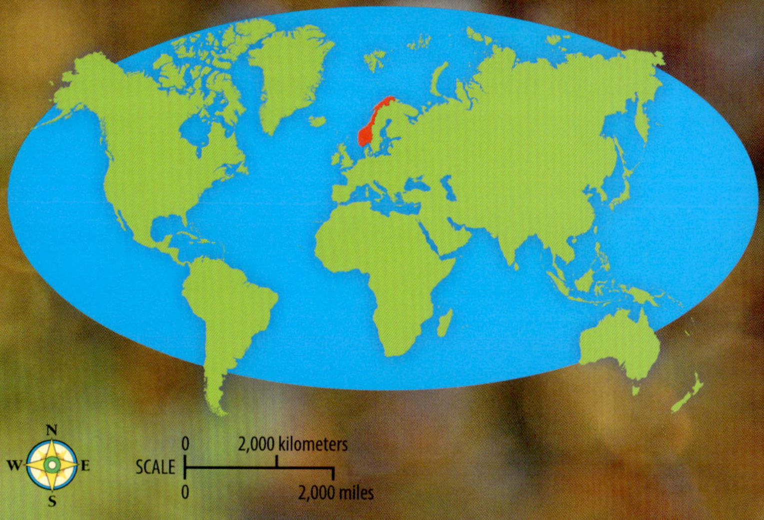

Norway

The Norwegian forest cat is known as *skogkatt* in its country of origin. The *skogkatt* is mentioned in some Norwegian **myths** from the Viking era. For instance, some stories say that the Norse goddess Freya traveled on a chariot pulled by two Norwegian forest cats.

Strong Legs and Long Fur

Norwegian forest cats are large, long-haired cats that look ready for a walk through the snowy woods. They come in many colors and patterns, including **tabby**, black, white, and gray. Norwegian forest cats have unique characteristics that help distinguish them from other cat breeds.

PAWS

Like the rest of its body, a Norwegian forest cat's paws are designed for cold weather. Tufts of fur help keep them warm.

EARS

Norwegian forest cat ears are very furry. Some cats may have extra tufts of hair, like those of a lynx, at the tips of their ears.

EYES

The large, almond-shaped eyes of Norwegian forest cats tilt upward. They come in many colors, including green, gold, copper, and blue.

Loyal Personalities

Norwegian forest cats enjoy being around people and will often follow their owners from room to room. However, Wegies are independent cats and like to make their own choices. They do enjoy cuddles, but they will choose when cuddle time is over. Often, Norwegian forest cats will choose one person as their favorite. Although they are not typically lap cats, they will sit near their owners. This means that the back of the couch might become a favorite **perch**.

Because they are calm and gentle, Wegies can get along well with children and other pets. They are happy to relax. They also enjoy play time and exploring. Norwegian forest cats are calm and talk with soft meows and chirps. They are a great choice for people who want a friendly, **affectionate** cat that does not require constant attention.

Happy and Playful

Norwegian forest cats have a long, kitten-like phase with plenty of playfulness and energy because they **mature** slowly. These cats also have a strong hunting **instinct** that they express by pouncing, chasing, and climbing. For example, they enjoy attacking feather wand toys that are waved in the air. Spending time playing with a Norwegian forest cat is an important daily bonding activity. It also provides the cat with plenty of exercise and fun.

In addition to playing with toys, Wegies like to climb and explore. Giving Norwegian forest cats safe, high places will help keep them entertained and healthy. They will be especially happy with a perch near a window that allows them to watch birds or squirrels.

Make a Cat Toy

New cat toys are a great way to entertain and engage a pet cat. Many of these can easily be made with simple and readily available household items. For example, one type of toy can be made with an empty toilet paper or paper towel roll.

To make the toy, first put some **catnip** inside the cardboard roll. Many cats are very sensitive to this herb. It will make the toy even more interesting for them. Next, seal both ends of the roll by folding them and taping them shut. Afterward, the cardboard roll can be decorated. For instance, adding feathers will stimulate a cat's hunting instinct. Finally, tie a string around the roll. The toy can now be pulled and wiggled or dangled in the air for a cat to chase.

Caring for Your Norwegian Forest Cat

Even though Norwegian forest cats have long, fluffy fur, their coats are not difficult to care for. These cats usually only require simple grooming to avoid tangles in their fur. Most of the time, Wegies do not **shed** very much. However, in the spring and fall, they will lose their warm winter undercoat. This process is called molting. While molting, Norwegian forest cats will need extra brushing. They may also need to be bathed.

Because Norwegian forest cats come from an area with a cold climate, they can overheat in hot weather. When it is hot, they need to always have a cool area available with plenty of shade. They also need access to fresh, clean water to remain **hydrated**.

Cat Supplies

Cat Tree Like most cats, Norwegian forest cats love to scratch and climb. They enjoy tall cat trees that include scratching posts wrapped in rope and platforms to climb on.

Brush Norwegian forest cats should be brushed at least once a week. Besides brushes, people can use combs with long **tines** to help detangle a Wegie's long fur.

Deshedding Tool A deshedding tool is used to remove the undercoat during molting. It helps reduce the amount of hair that a Norwegian forest cat sheds.

Nail Trimmers Norwegian forest cat claws should be trimmed every two weeks. Only the sharp claw tips need to be trimmed. Cutting too far might damage the **quick** and cause bleeding.

Healthy Norwegian Forest Cats

With good care, Norwegian forest cats are usually healthy. As with any pet cat, they should be taken to a **veterinarian** for regular checkups. They should also be kept indoors and fed a healthy diet. Norwegian forest cats enjoy a mix of dry and wet food.

To avoid gum disease, a Norwegian forest cat's teeth should be brushed daily. Like many other **purebreds**, these cats are prone to certain health problems. For example, Wegies can have problems with their hip and knee joints. They may also suffer from skin and heart diseases. Responsible cat **breeders** can help breed kittens who are less at risk for many health problems. Before selecting a kitten, cat owners should ask breeders plenty of questions and make sure they are choosing the right pet for their family.

Average Weight of Pet Cats

If You Like Norwegian Forest Cats...

Some cats resemble Norwegian forest cats in appearance. Others share a similar **disposition**. If you like Norwegian forest cats, here are some other cat breeds you might enjoy.

American Bobtail

Like Norwegian forest cats, American bobtails look rugged and ready for adventure. However, American bobtails have very short tails. They are loyal, playful, and affectionate. They like to play games, including hide and seek.

Maine Coon

Maine coons are large cats with long coats and tails. The Norwegian forest cat is believed to be their distant relative. Maine coons get along well with humans and other pets. They like to be silly and can even be trained to play fetch.

Persian

Persians and Norwegian forest cats have long, fluffy fur. Both cat breeds are also calm and friendly. However, Persians require more maintenance and need daily brushing. They are less adventurous than Norwegian forest cats, too. This makes them good lap cats.

Ragdoll

Another cat with long, fluffy fur, the ragdoll is as big as the Norwegian forest cat. Cats of this breed can weigh up to 20 pounds (9 kg). Ragdoll cats have mellow personalities. They love to cuddle. They also welcome being picked up and petted.

Siamese

Like the Norwegian forest cat breed, the Siamese breed has been around for hundreds of years. However, Siamese cats differ greatly from Wegies in appearance. A Siamese cat has short fur and a specific color pattern. Its body is light in color, while its face, ears, and paws are dark.

Norwegian Forest Cat Quiz

1
When did the Norwegian forest cat become the official cat breed of Norway?

2
What are Norwegian forest cats called in Norway?

3
Which cat weighs only 4 to 8 pounds (1.8 to 3.6 kg) on average?

4
How often should a Norwegian forest cat's teeth be brushed?

5
What is a Norwegian forest cat's warm inner layer of fur called?

6
When did a breeding pair of Norwegian forest cats first come to the United States?

7
Which parts of a cat's claws should be trimmed?

8
How long can Norwegian forest cats live?

Answers:
1. In the 1950s **2.** *Skogkatt* **3.** Singapura **4.** Daily **5.** An undercoat **6.** In 1979 **7.** Only the sharp tips **8.** Up to 16 years

Key Words

affectionate: showing love or care
breed: a group of animals with similar characteristics and family history
breeders: people who raise and sell young animals
catnip: an herb with a smell that cats enjoy
climates: general weather conditions in specific areas
disposition: personality
hydrated: having enough water in the body
instinct: a natural behavior with which animals are born
mature: grow up
myths: traditional stories, usually about supernatural or fantastic beings
native: place of origin
pedigree registry: an organization in charge of certifying that individual animals belong to a specific breed
perch: a high place to sit
purebreds: an animal that comes from parents each belonging to a specific breed
quick: the area below the growing part of a nail that contains nerves and blood vessels
ruff: long fur around the neck
shed: lose fur
tabby: gray or brown with dark stripes
tines: the teeth of a comb
undercoat: short fur beneath an animal's outer layer of fur
vermin: animals seen as pests, such as rats
veterinarian: a doctor for animals
Vikings: ancient people who lived in the northernmost area of Europe and were known for sea travel

Index

Get the best of both worlds.

AV2 bridges the gap between print and digital.

The expandable resources toolbar enables quick access to content including **videos**, **audio**, **activities**, **weblinks**, **slideshows**, **quizzes**, and **key words**.

Animated videos make static images come alive.

Resource icons on each page help readers to further **explore key concepts**.

Published by Lightbox Learning Inc.
276 5th Avenue
Suite 704 #917
New York, NY 10001
Website: www.openlightbox.com

Library of Congress Cataloging-in-Publication Data available upon request.

ISBN: 978-1-7911-5624-4 (hardcover)
ISBN: 978-1-7911-5625-1 (softcover)
ISBN: 978-1-7911-5626-8 (multi-user eBook)

Printed in Guangzhou, China
1 2 3 4 5 6 7 8 9 0 27 26 25 24 23

042023
101122

Project Coordinator: Sara Cucini
Designer: Terry Paulhus
Layout: Jean Faye Marie Rodriguez

Photo Credits
Every reasonable effort has been made to trace ownership and to obtain permission to reprint copyright material. The publisher would be pleased to have any errors or omissions brought to its attention so that they may be corrected in subsequent printings.
The publisher acknowledges Alamy, Dreamstime, Getty Images, and Shutterstock as its primary image suppliers for this title.